YOU SHOULD FALL IN LOVE FOREVER AT LEAST ONCE *EVERYDAY*

A Book of Poetry & Lyrics

By

Bruce R. Sanford

authorHOUSE

A Book of Poetry & Lyrics

AuthorHouse™
1663 Liberty Drive
Bloomington, IN 47403
www.authorhouse.com
Phone: 1 (800) 839-8640

Published by AuthorHouse 10/26/2016

ISBN: 978-1-5246-4108-5 (sc)
ISBN: 978-1-5246-4107-8 (e)

Library of Congress Control Number: 2016915674

Print information available on the last page.

Dedicated to My Father/My Teacher

My Mother/My Guide

Three candles glow to spread their warmth

A fire burns to guide their way

A torch is held and carried on

In hope that I might also lead . . .

Table of Contents

LXXVIII. WITHIN WITHOUT

: Shoot me down

LXXIX. YOU SHOULD FALL IN LOVE FOREVER

AT LEAST ONCE

EVERYDAY / #1

: She walks by, so beautifully shy

LXXX. YOU SHOULD FALL IN LOVE FOREVER

AT LEAST ONCE

EVERYDAY / #2

: Sweet Melinda, I cannot forget

LXXXI. YOU SHOULD FALL IN LOVE FOREVER

AT LEAST ONCE

EVERYDAY / #3

: And as we say in so many ways

LXXXII. THE YEAR OF "SWEET SIXTEEN" + 1000

2016 To 3016

: Be in love with the future.

LXXXIII. A WORTHY PERSON

: You will surely meet

LXXXIV. POSTSCRIPT: IT ALL COMES FULL CIRCLE

: Do you think that people are trying

ROMAN NUMERAL GUIDE: I=1, V=5, X=10, L=50, C=100, D=500, M=1000, IV=4 (1 before 5), IX=9 (1 before 10), XIV=14 (10+4), XIX=19 (10+9), XXI=21, XXIV=24 (20+4), XXIX=29 (20+9), XXXIX=39 (30+9), XL=40 (10 before 50), XLI=41, XLIV=44 (40+4), XLIX=49 (40+9), LI=51, LIV=54 (50+4), LV=55, LIX=59 (50+9), LXXX=80, LXXXIV=84, CI=101, CIV=104, CIX=109, CD=400 (100 before 500), CM=900 (100 before 1000), MCM=1900 (1000+900), MM=2000, MMXVI=2016.

I.

ABSTAIN

Can love fall in behind a lost embrace
Can love begin to warm a sad, sad face
Can love hold fast
Can love be first and stay beyond an endless last?

Can you believe in love accusing us
Can you agree that love's abusing us
Can you hold fast
Can you belong to me and stay my endless last?

Can you believe
Can love fall in
Can you agree
Can love begin
Can you and love hold fast
Can you and love at first belong, then stay an endless last?

If I try harder now that you know how I feel
If I go farther in believing that we're real
If I admit
our love can grow and stay aglow more brightly lit
will you get off along with me?

I met you on that traveling show of clouds
You found me floating happy, high, around a crowd
I kissed you numbly – though you swelled my thoughts
You held me tightly – though you knew no strength.

We found excuses to be free and found our love a lie
We hadn't really met at all – until we saw each other back on board
Our love inverted what we were – and hopes have shown us dreams
but can we make insertions known – and mend our separate seams?

Can we believe in us without excuse
Can we agree with us without misuse
Can we hold fast
Can we belong to us alone and not be ruled?

(cont'd)

Can we believe
Can love fall in
Can we hold fast
Can love be real
Can you and I be real
Can you and I begin
Can we and love at first belong – then stay an endless last?

II.

ACCIDENTAL LIFE

Eating air, lying in space
Hung up in the middle
Snuck up from behind

Drinking anti's, sucking in sleep
Exercising waiting
Missing my love

    Now I'm afraid of what comes from behind
    and what shows from the sides
    Control isn't owning the right-of-way
    It's giving is up when it's taken away.

More in touch with loving much--
more than we know
Strong in line with living blind—
when we're apart
My heart couldn't ache more than needing you
late in my loneliness.
You live in a vacuum just loving and living—
my heart beats your time.

    You ask to believe and then think you're deceived—
    in a trick.
    But never apart from the spirits of heart—
    when kept beating.
    A knock on the door in a life meant for more—
    I should stay.

But arm me with faith in a spirit awake to my doubt.

When fright shows an eye of my love--no goodbyes—
I've been Blessed,
not only in life and my love's standing right,
but in love with a treasure to love me.

III.

A LOST YEAR

The day is long. The road is wide
and I have strayed between feeling them side by side.
Curbs don't touch and I don't see much
since the distance is way out of sight and rush.

       Head in my hand
       Chin in my palm
       Eyes looking downward
       Still farther than seen

       I've skipped my May to September
       and April through October slipped by;
       but now that I've found November around,
       my March and December are gone.

And so another year of my life goes by
And so another plan of my life lies
buried behind and below winter's thaw
and cold February looms tall.

IV.

AMERICANS

I'm not a raging patriot,
And I'm not complaining to be free;
BUT take caution if you tread on me.
My middle finds no gaps to be
upon your quick and snuff it out.
My Generation Knocks About !

Come fast, loose ends and untied thoughts—
minorities not left to rot.
We'll stand and gather all to one—
outsiders thinking that we'd run.
We need not coax out unity.
They'd see us swell beyond our seas.

Take bitter fights within our walls
We're healing wounds, though cuts will call
our seething, foaming, pride to hide
deep pain among us. Others chide
they cannot live together there;
but do not tease or test us, or
our common heart will lay you bare.
Our Generations Knock About!

Look to our land and people then,
if you should stand and wonder when
we'd fall, give in, or break the bend.
We'd laugh you off, back to the shores,
and even farther, if you pour
your power above our vigilant doors.
Our Generations Knock About!

Take note! Don't Dote on all our strife.
We're throbbing, bobbing, full of life.
We've got some growing pains to solve;
but our healthy signs will soon evolve
into one life, one body all.
Our Generations All Stand Tall!

(cont'd)

Take sturdy growth. Heal from within.
The outside always shades what's in;
but truth is bright. They see our sins.
So let's admit them and begin
to take our bruises, scars, and blood
away from faces caked with mud.

America we know must stand Alone !

But to isolate? We can't do that!
We stand on Freedom's Flag of Faith!
Let history repeat itself:
Our country grows its own relief.
We'll stand as one, divided not --
together if we face a shot.
So think before you press too far:

Americans Will Knock About !

V.

APATHY AND DECAY

If you want to hear the wind you'll have to turn into your mind.

The wind cannot be heard without your waiting for its sound.

If you want to ride the wave you'll have to get on all your dreams;

for a wave just will not wander through a person's well planned schemes.

To hear the wind and ride the wave to where you've been on other days ---

To go along for nothing when you'd choose another course ---

You're foolish not to make the choice to move out on your own.

Don't wait to hear the wind come up and make its endless sound.

Don't ride the wave to nowhere when the choice is yours to where you're bound. Not You. Go.

VI.

ATTICA/WATERGATE/WASHINGTON/EMAILGATE/DALLAS

Too Many Have Left Their Homes To Rule in Neighborhood Castles:

Today's a slow encumbered pace
for many sweat and die.
Today's a fear engulfing us
for many need to lie.

To know of lost and yet be free
to live within the wall
To think of them who reach to us
yet doubting when set free.

It's not a lie to call disease
a known great quantity.
We're caught also, choked by the bars
tormenting us, and more by far
those caught by you and me.

"Relieve me, save me, set me free.
Unbind my body from the tree!"
We're stopped and stumped—Accused Guilty
by victims we're ashamed to see.

Don't call on me you hypocrites.
I'm guilty! So are you!
Don't panic in the wake of fear.
The time is here! It's here! It's here!

Rebellion sets the stage for death.
We gather all our arms.
Strike each one down who dares to tread
too close to sounding the alarm.

No, don't conceal your ignorance.
You know we're all to blame.
Destroy a human dog and brain.
Destroy the weak, for when they came
they made you see yourself in me,
quite conscious of your game.   (cont'd)

VI. ATTICA/WATERGATE/WASHINGTON/EMAILGATE/DALLAS (cont'd)

We harm ourselves—Full circle's come.
We run around again.
Let them come out? We can't do that.
They'll tell us we're in hell, in hell.
The devil rings for us, not them.
The fire burns outside the den!

The Chief? He gathers all who'll suck
the juice from bowels within the muck.
And guardians all, we hold the club
above the filth we will not scrub,
for coming clean, we can't afford.
It threatens loss of what we horde!

Humanity, I spit on you and doing so, spit on me.
We can't erase hypocrisy, when conscience is the key.
We say that Satan's down below?
You Fool! He's you and me !
He never laughed so hard as we.
We thought we clubbed him blow by blow.

The grouping's clear. We're after us !
We'll get us too: And When We Do,
we'll fight like hell to answer us:
"Oh, Why have we?. . . Did we?. . . What Can We Do? . . .

But dying bravely, bending bars,
we'll bury us with open scars.
And Time Will Read:

WE PURGED OURSELVES AND DIED WITHIN OUR MAN-MADE HELL!

or

Time Will Read:

WE PURGED OURSELVES AND LIVED TO BREED A FUTURE FOR
OUR KIDS TO BREATHE A HEALTHY BREATH OF CHILDREN
LEADING FAIRNESS, ENERGY, AND LOVE FOR ALL.

AMEN

VII.

A VOW

And with the vow

That comes from depths

Beyond the heart

Beyond the soul

Life and death never end. I offer you infinity.

VIII.

BE YOURSELF

If you plan for it, you're thinking about it.

If you're thinking about it, you're watching it happen.

If you're watching it happen, it cannot be natural:

Loving, Talking, Singing, Playing, Working. . .

Breathing

BIRTH CONTROL

Too many kids and too little care

Too much conceit and too little love

Superfluous indulgence and minimal awareness

Irascible provocation with irrelevant meditation

Choose Life Control

X.

BOILING POINT: 212/100 WATER

Poor man's got to worry 'bout the place he's got to go.
Easy man's got less to care 'bout things he doesn't know.
Social man's a moving force, existing in us all;
but no one knows until he's faced disaster growing tall.

Middle man's a liar, thinking not much touches him;
but hate and fear and suffering come boiling to the brain.
Then watch the flow come over, burning all within the flood.
Can't run, can't hide, can't even cry when the boiling's in the blood.

Listen to the pain, we fools, whose pleasure seems so safe.
It grows, infectious, rooted deep, devouring as it rakes
the hungry, starving, tortured souls who fight to cling to life.
The clamoring we will not hear, but watch our petty strife.

"Oh, Quiet them! Reduce their pain!" We yell it from on high.
"Why do they shout and bother us, complain as if to die
without some help, humane concern? -- Well, throw the dog a bone."
"But, make sure that they share it, break it, even take some home."

Ha! Home, you say! And where is that? -- A poor beleaguered cry
cannot erode the walls of time and apathy grown high.
But only shouts of forceful, painful, blood washed on our hands
will cause a hearing, seeing, smelling touch of tasting pain.

I can't go home! You can't turn back! - - to places they have not
been free to buy or pay to see, regardless of their lot.
Reduce my guilt! Accept your shame! Their victories we cannot blame.

It's all too clear. It's all too plain. We need to heat the flames
to warm the heartbeat of mankind and power the powers to drive
machines to block despair and burn the candles to the healing point.

XI.

CHANGING LOVE

Think back to the gold
then look to the dark
and take off the robe.
Now notice the hair.
It's turned dark now,
though shining bright
the carpet holds no strands of gold.

Think back to the many
and seek out the few.
Complain too much
then try to explain
the dark combined
then overcame
with equal brightness, old and new.

Think back to the length
of the time gold was one,
rejecting the sun
and burning the night.
Warm love is a star,
foreshadowing
equal love and missing strength.

Think back to the taste
sinking down to the light
draining off in the bog
running freely again.
Passing day through the night
knowing dark into light.
With one far away, the other one stays.

Think back to be now.
Look up to be come.
Ask what now to do
when at once they run.
Dark light to be one
and fear not to please.
Black strength and time is a glowing line
where strong darkness and time, soon brightness finds.

XII.

CHOSEN LONELINESS

To whom am I supposed to talk
    when I cut off all the strings?

To whom am I supposed to cling
    when I let go of everything?

Of whom am I supposed to think
    when I say you'll have to go?

On whom am I supposed to look back
    when I've written all I know?

    "Boy, you're gonna get it!
        Boy, you're gonna pay the price!
        You'll be sorry and you'll see you're wrong
        when no one's here, then you will see
        how everything is thrown away !"

What am I supposed to do
when free and no one speaks?

What am I supposed to do
when hours and days grow into weeks?

What am I supposed to do
when words no longer answer doubts?

What am I supposed to do
if I should want to turn about?

    "Boy, you're gonna get it!
        Boy, you're gonna pay the price!
        You'll be sorry and you'll see you're wrong
        when no one's here, then you will see
        how everything is thrown away !"

XIII.

COUNSELING TRICKS

Sure my clock works ! It just tells the same time all the time.

My thoughts wander by me
where they used to want to try me
while my darkness crept around me
and my shadow said goodbye.

I couldn't see to love me
so I asked about above me
where the light was s'posed to blind me
in my vacuum filled with dark.

Of course I love warm weather ! What's that got to do with spring?

My feathery existence
causes questions of resistence
from the mouths of those persistent
in their search into my cave.

I haven't told a soul about
what I cannot tell you about
and since it's only me about
I'll keep it from myself.

I didn't say I wouldn't take a life. What's that got to do with death?

My spending time or lending time
is not a means of ending time.
There's only time for mending time
that's broken by the bend, in time.

I couldn't phone or go alone,
so I began to stay at home,
not waiting for that heavy moan,
but hearing why it calls.

Yes, but if I were rich, I wouldn't know what the word means.

XIV.

DEFINITION

Life is like a wave on the ocean.

It is a creation far off somewhere and only love is aware,
but as it approaches shore, yet still at a distance,
people begin to take notice.

They watch it swell/rise/crest/break/gather itself
again and again, and then as it reaches the shore - - -
it's creation perhaps becomes

A large wave breaking beautifully smooth
A large wave ending with a crash and thunder - - - devastating
A medium wave that rolls into shore comfortably, or
reaches its own kind of devastating power, or
a small wave that merely blends into the sand,
without much jostling or rumble or fuss,

or you as your unique self.

And so - - - life ends.

DESTINY

I'm down to my last dollar bill
I'm down to my last buck of luck
I'm down to my chin
where my shoulders begin
to be drooping and slumping again.

I'm out of my last breath of hope
I've started to stop my descent
I've looked at my future
and laughed at my past
but haven't seen fit to fade out.

I'm up to my nose in arrears
Nobody to call or give cheers
The bills left today
can't be paid in that way
Oh, laughter, don't give me away.

There's no one to talk about gone
There's only one life going on
My loneliness stands
like a bucket of sand
full moisture, big weight under hand.

What happens is coming along
Can't see it until it's been gone
Time's got me a scheme
so there's no use to dream
I've been taken care of it seems.

DON'T LET ME FORGET

How should I remember
    what I used to tell myself I never could forget.
How can I remember
    things I never thought about just passing through my head.
How could I forget
    when we used to tell each other: "Never let me go !"
How can I forget
    days filled, all with playful times, no serious doubts of love.
Let me be. Oh, why
    must I keep remembering forgotten things gone by.
Let me be. Oh, how
    could I have ever thought I'd think about her now.
Think about her now?
    How can I remember things so far beyond and passed?
Ask myself and then
    lie about forgotten love, yet still remembered now.
How should I think now?
    My thoughts all crumble on the path I'm following to her.
What do I hear now?
    I'm spending time in thoughts gone by, to stay away.
Let me be. Oh, why
    must I keep remembering forgotten things gone by.
Let me be. Oh, how
    could I have thought I'd think about her now.
Mix me up. I beg you.
    Let me come out puzzled, with no answers in my head.
Turn me round and over.
    Tell me that I don't know what I'm thinking. That is that.
Say that I'm all wrong.
    Please tell me to go back to sleep. It's only been a dream.
Please do not let me speak.
    Don't let me tell you what I think. I worry more and more.
Please allow me not to ramble
    or I'll wander deeper into further more.
Go back to sleep and remember.

XVII.

EVERY OTHER HER

I wake up and I think of you.
I start the day. I think of her.
She's far away. You're close to me.
I hold you tight. She set me free.

I talk to her. I speak your name.
I mention love and feel the blame.
She's won a heart. Compassion starts.
You tell of futures far apart.

I sleep with you. I dream of her.
I drink your taste and pour her pain.
I go with you. She waits for me.
You give me you. She took my name.

I hear your voice. She speaks to me.
I read your words. I hear her thoughts.
I write you notes. She sings to me.
I cast you off. She clings to me.

She's been in love. You come to it.
You see romance. She lives a dance.
You're strong and calm. She's been there long.
Days live with you. Time fills her glance.

XVIII.

EXPONENTIAL TIMING

I'm at three to the third
and to speak in a word,
I've lived.
  I've had three in my one
  and I think that I'm done,
  I've loved.
    I've had one out of three
    and there's still more for me,
    I've worked.
I'd like three to the third with one more to make four,
live and love with my work, nothing more.
I'm at one equal part with two more yet to start,
maybe thirty time three if there's heart.

  We are months between three,
  and in years, add square three,
  we are born.
    You're at two times square three,
    times one more and that's me,
    we've begun.
      By your seven and three,
      three would multiply me,
      we are free.
We'll be different square three, and there's just you and me,
live and love, multiply and be free.
Cubing three times a three, brings you closer to me,
melting cubes, rounding squares, you and me.

  One in three has been taught.
  Zero power I'm not.
  I've learned.
    Two for three is a note
    written following strokes.
    I have sung.
      Zero power for me
      is the one with all three.
      I have helped.
Operations of time, fusing distance with line
and a word in a square two times three.
Leading players to play with my square three to love,
living distance, our measure of time.

XIX.

FAREWELL TO MASKS AND MINSTRELS

Tis a while ago he started learning of his plans.
Tis a while ago he started searching through the sand.
His heart had lost a love he'd known.
Now it's a sadness, greatly grown, and sinking where he stands.

His dreams have all been cuckolded.
His schemes have buckled down his youth.
He's lost direction. Where's he going?
Perhaps he'll catch an "out brief light".

To screw his courage 'til it sticks, erasing dam'ed spots---
And wherefore art thou roams his life, inside his maddening
brain.
To be himself or not to be a lonely lover 'til he dies,
his lover's kerchief's long been seized.
He's had no one, no where to cry.

Come back sweet love. Come back fair game.
         His kingdom's horse has died unborn.
His flesh to flesh n'er gained a pound.
         A dusty strength has left him torn.

         So, Out! - he says - Brief candle, Out!
         "I've lived too long, so long, no longer
         shall I play my error's joke.
         My blindness yields to pluck my sight
         before I sleep my sleepless night."

His "while ago" has planned his start.
His sand has filled its glass. -- He thinks.
His hand can hold no lover more.
And sadness bids farewell and adieu -- at last.

XX.

FOOEY

Don't live your life in a nutshell.

Happiness in not a peanut.

GIVING UP ?

I've got to stop applying
for entrances to love.
My application's been denied.
I've tried to force my way.

My resignation's not been sought.
I've not been told to leave,
But time and pain destroy the game.
The loser's at my door.

Take this last application.
Try now. Apply and check.
Can yes or no be used to score
sad faces at the door?

If I'm rejected, I'll concede.
I'll never knock again.
I'll go away and face the days
while sadness tries to grin.

No! I will NOT give up.
She is applying for me too.
God has it under control.
Yes! In His Time. Not mine.

GRANDMA'S PASSED

Light a candle for your grandma.
Light a candle for she's gone.
Light a candle so she'll have some light
to find her way toward home.

Say a prayer goodbye to grandma.
Say a thought you've left for her.
Say a word of warmth with candle light
to guide her as she goes.

Think about the life she's had
and think about her fun.
Be glad that she is happier
and joining one upon the run.

Thank her spirit that remains with you.
Thank her life that's mixed with yours.
Think about it as you see her flame
in the candles glowing at the gates.

So, light a candle. Feel her warmth.
Light a candle. Feel her strength.
Lift her spirit with your own,
since all continues, never alone.

XXIII.

HAPPY BLUES

Excuse me if I'm laughing; and excuse me if my eyes are wet.
Excuse me 'cause I'm high on being happy now.
My friends all hold me down with love.
My foes have flown away.
We've met the push and held it back.
The rush is off for space.

I've pointed somewhere else for strength.
The crucifying's over now.
The stones have fallen from my back.
The nails have withered
and my arms are strong.

I'm not in a line at all because I'm curving as they come.
I'm safe to be your friend and come to something new.
It's down. It's up. I've no excuse.
It's down. It's up. It's all around.
There's no excuse. The reason's clear.
It's called the happy blues.

XXIV.

HE DIED A RICH MAN

All that he carried was thirty-six cents
the day he checked on death.

A penny for his thoughts

A dime for a paper to read of his passing

And a quarter for a shine to see his last
appearance.

IDOLS ARE QUOTED

Big ears, little ears
    All to hear you speak

Big mouths, little mouths
    Listen to you leak

Information you had said
    But wished they'd kept secret

No matter what you do
    No matter what you say

No matter good or bad
    They spoke the words you said.

What can you do? You can't be mad.
    Their truth has made you smile --- or sad.

XXVI.

I KNEW YOU BEST

What do you live and laugh for?
For what do you cry and love?
Do you really have something to do?
Can you really have something to say?

      It seems that when I walk on air
      I've got the feeling of not being where
      I really am or want to be.
      It just fades away from reality.

Sometimes when I talk to you you're not around.
Sometimes when I walk with you you're off the ground.
Sometimes when I've need for you, you can't be found.
Sometimes when I'm loving you you're tightly bound.

      But when I'm far away from you
      you're lost and lonely.
      You're ready to crack and you beg me back.
      Is it me you crave or are you afraid
      when you've burst your cocoon
      and you cannot bear it?

To be alone --- to live with yourself
To be with yourself and yet not there
To talk to yourself and get no reply
To walk with someone who isn't there
To need someone and no one cares
To love someone --- or think you do;

      But you're really afraid that it's only you.

XXVII.

IN MEMORY OF KAY

Tell her to plant a sycamore tree.

Plant it deep and plant it for me.

I will grow and think of days that will be.

And I'll know she is coming to, reaching for, speaking to me.

XXVIII.

IN THE RUNNING . . . DID YOU SHOW?
MIDDLE OF THE ROAD

Where's your place in the human race?
How much space do you trace?

Through your living you take up a space
and the line before you can be traced.
Still, deny that you're part human race
and be spared from the must-take-a-place.

Say what you have to say and be brief.
The time isn't yours to delay.
Grow, since you have to be gone.
The days linger by, short and long.

Be where you're needed and seen.
Go only where no one's between.
Stay back if there's no need to bore
and pick from beyond evermore.

Stay out of the middle ends two,
above argument, false and true.
Speak only to those who are you,
and safely you'll die when it's through.

You can have your place. It's not for me.
You'll be safe and there'll be no disgrace.
But the middle's no place to be sure.
Stretch farther than safely secure.

XXIX.

IT TAKES ALL KINDS

It Takes one heck of a lot of frustration,

    with open-minded thinking,

    unprejudiced behavior,

    fair play and self-respect

        to live in a society that relies

        upon a stability based on the belief

        in the equality of ALL KINDS !

    It's a big lie !

Very few are open, unprejudiced, play fair, or even
have their self-respect.

But. It could happen.

XXX.

LIFE IS A MULTIPLE CHOICE/COMPLETION TEST

Once Upon A Time . . .

Rabbits . . . . .CURTAIN RODS . . . .

ASHES . . . . ENGINES . . . . MRS. . . . .

LUMBER . . . . FAR AWAY . . . .

. . . . .YES . . . . WALLS . . . . .KEROSENE . .

MIRRORS . . . . . CANDLES . . . . WHY . . . .

. . . . CHALK . . . . PERSIAN . . . . .FORK . . .

. . . VICTORY . . . . . . .STATUE . . . . .PILLOW . . . .

. . KEYS . . . . .ELECTRIC . . . . SATIN . . .

CANE . . . . HURRICANE . . . . . . STRAP . . . . . FUMES . . . . . .

. . . . CLIMAX . . . . LONG DISTANCE . .

. . . . ORIGINAL . . . . .LISTEN . . . . . . .OUTSIDE . . . . NOW . .

MELTED . . . . LIE . . . . SPEAKER . . . .

. . . . . .WRONG . . . . .NEVER . . . . FROZEN . .

. . . . .READ BLUE . . . . Shelf.

The End.

XXXI.

LOVELY BESIDE ME - #3

She slips in calmly
She silently asks me – ok?
She smiles down warmly
She sits down and begins to stay.

She reads quite gently
She doesn't devour in a rage
She needs most surely
She's satisfied missing a page.

She looks away softly
She knows she's alone and alone
She glances back shyly
She's looking for feeling at home.

She speaks with her movements
She's sorry if she's been a bore
She walks with knowing
She's questioning thoughts of before.

She's gone from staying
She hesitates waiting for signs
She's gone. I'm praying
She's sure to know there are two minds.

She's gone/being looked for
Oh, why and why – Why was I blind?
She's gone. I've lost her.
She's disappeared within my mind.

She is always there.

XXXII.

MAKE-UP LESSON

When I was a young man, I suffered my innocence.
I lived with my guilt if I had punctured a heart
or caused someone pain; and the child of my trust
and the child of my gust became mixed with the
children of truth and faith.

But when I became a grown man --- tame
and began to play the adult wo/man's game,
I learned how to doubt and give no wo/man my trust.
I met with untruths in adult wo/man's lust,
for the friendship adult men and women express
leads mostly to pastimes without an address.

For no grown-up times you.
S/He only unwinds you,
and finding your core,
s/he exposes and lines you
within her/his desires if s/he needs you to be
of use to abuse you
and then to refuse you
unless you can help her/him for growth in her/his greed.

So children be heard.
Make them know they're absurd.
When your games are your own
you play fair !
For growing brings life
ever closer, alone.
So prepare to play fair when you're grown.

All that I learned as a kid – I began to forget
as an adult:
                    Expecting the truth !
                    Trusting in people !
                    Depending on leaders !

But now that I search for the truths on my own
to find trust in the ones I embrace,
I find hope and full faith that they're there
to be loved and relied upon by their grace.

XXXIII.

MAYBE I'M RIGHT

You are remembered much longer by people if you do not stay in touch or bother them too often, and therefore keep them wondering about you, and perhaps interested and/or intrigued by you. For the minute you notify them of your situation, needs, ideas, opinions, they begin to think that maybe you're up to something they might like to know, and you are once again placed in their thoughts.

Too Negative?

My friendship is forever !

Never doubt it !

XXXIV.

MECHANICAL FUTURE

The lizard cries --- antagonize
the peasants and the ants.
The crickets weep and rub our sleep
between their legs and pegs.

We worms, we lie awaiting day
the oozing will erupt,
and wipe the slime across mankind
to stop the growth of eggs.

The weasel hangs in limpid drains
of women's holiness /
Then pushing power across the hour,
our night engulfs the ruin.

For why bring forth another court /
another darkness feast?
The snake of life, entombe'd strife /
though stars, we cannot cheat.

Then mock the cockroach combing place
when candles lose their heat.
Watch through the distance, blindly filled
With tunnels trying to sleep.

For robots, we, will antlike be,
And tubes will hold our being /
With droning choices for our work /
The fungus is our food.

XXXV.

MOTHER TEACHES QUIETLY

All I want to say is that we love this woman called Mother.

She's full of understanding
deep with love and faith in me.
There's nothing she won't listen to.
There's patience 'til I'm through.
She's heard me lie. She's heard me boast.
She's laughed at all my jokes.
I've hurt her so she's had to cry
and maybe doubt I loved her most.
With no excuse she still refused
to doubt me, turn away.
She knows me in. I learn her out.
I always know what she's about.

We must admit we've tested her.
She's never let us down.
We're not so clever, though we think
she's not known all we've lost and found.
We grow below her, yet we know
she wants us to be free.
She's teaching us by checking us,
refusing us some things to be.
We're proud of her, and of us too,
for knowing that she likes us.
She sees we're happy and she smiles
behind us and inside.
We're part of her. She fits with us.
We're friends. We talk. We know.

We've hurt her and she's healed the wound.
She never turned us down.
She painfully accepted us
and faces left the ground.
She grew with us and grows for us,
together going along.
Her smile's returned; we've salved the burn;
some irritation's round.
Her eyes meet ours with distant pain,
yet love refuses stain.

(cont'd)

MOTHER TEACHES QUIETLY   (cont'd)

Though general this thought may read,
specific is its aim.
I've left apology below
the need to say the same.
A mother knows what's gone beyond
the spoken word or thought.
She simply sees the future
passing faster than a dot.
She therefore covers past with faith
in future's prideful lot,
And we go on by knowing that
our mothers/fathers love through us into the world.

All we want to say is that we love this woman called Mother.

Postscript:
No need explaining of the line
we thought about or wrote.
For mothers read between the lines
composing special notes.
And realizing what we've said
they sigh and lift a thought
of how no mention need be made,
as time engulfs the dot.

XXXVI.

MY WANT

I want to be myself.
I want to know what I will be, a long long time ago.

I want to know what I have been, a longer time from now.

> No one the same
> No more to blame
> I want to be myself.

I want to know what you were like, when I will fall in love.
I want to know what love will give me, when I used to care.

> No one for late
> No more to wait
> I want to be myself.

I want to know how long you'll need before we wind and wind.
I want to know how long I'll follow what I left behind.

> No one to pray
> No more to say
> I want to be myself.

I want to know how you will lead, when you follow me.
I want to know what I have said, when I will call for you.

> I want to be myself.
> Just you to love
> So far above
> My want to be myself.

XXXVII.

NEW BELIEF

I have always lived with the thought and hope that one day
    I would become well-known, famous, popular, rich, and
    any other frivolous description of the universal wish of
    members of free, competitive, dogmatic, suppressed, or
    otherwise normally different societies of the world.

I often planned how I would treat my acclaim:

?

However, now I find that it is better to be deep, dark, and quiet,
    but not necessarily secret, in order to plan and be heard.

P.S.   The secret to success is as follows:
    "Not to have a pot to pee in, but have
    Faith that you will make it pay anyway!"
    & reach paydirt !

Just Be Yourself

(And you can quote me !)

XXXVIII.

NO INTERFERENCE

So when I want to be alone
I come to You.
Your privacy allows me lost
In thoughts that only You dare see.
My loneliness is safe in You.
Your presence seeks my company.
We're finding shelter, lonely ones.
We want to be together, free.

XXXIX.

NOT ENOUGH

I call you everyday --- That's not enough.
I see you every other day --- That's not enough.
And weekends we're together morn to night --- That's not enough.

I lie awake and think of you.
I want you close to me.
I think of you when I awake.
I want you there to say: "Stay here with me."

You come with me. We touch and love --- That's not enough.
We talk of time, of future plans.
Emotion begs, while wisdom drags.

And when the future comes to us,
we'll see our way to closer ties each day.
Those days will pass, we'll love still more.
We'll live two lives as one, and when we're through ---

That's Not Enough !

XL.

NOT TOO PROFOUND

You cannot show me more a love
    I've not already seen.
And I cannot admit there's less
    than that you call my own.

I cannot make my get-away
since I cannot deny it's you.
I've never been so far away
as now when we're a breath apart
and cannot taste each other's warmth.
Instead --- We wait --- We pray --- We dream.

One thing is for certain.
One thing is for sure.
It always will be us.
It always will be more.

A breath apart is more heartbreaking than farewell.
It comes so near and we're so helpless to move closer.

A love like ours will never die
And as the time goes by . . .

Keep breathing, my lovely . . .
We will breathe us into us forever . . .

XLI.

OBSTACLES

If s/he weren't there and were out of my way
I could do a whole week's work
in a single day.

It's happens.
Es verdad.
C'est vrai.
It's true.

XLII.

OLYMPUS ZWEI UND SIEBZIG

They're dead! They're gone! Down the ancient run
of the flame, to the grave, turned to blood.
Struck beyond nation's bonds
Shot the rounds of pain, lying prone
to the host, steeped in shame.
No one's fault, no one vaults
over springs now awry with despair.

Tree of man, seen a sham
Born of brave, made a slave
to a stranger, still barely wound out.
Peaceful runs now are done.
Torches lit for a war still ahead.
Made to be without choice
by the innocent voice,
haunting whispers go on facing death.

Questions hope, answers slope
to the negative after we think
hopeless thoughts, worthless loss,
doubting positive ways to go on;
but the tears through the silence
bring the mirrors shining backwards,
crossing borders based on hate and seen as hell.

So the games go on and some fail to respect
lines of family ties facing dead dreams.
And boasting pride erupts into phlegm,
choking and rising into spit
on the races still ahead in the line.
As the coffins emerge on the future,
sand will dust them warmly
and admit them to a golden braid of ludicricy.

Kill! And Kill! And fill the bill!
The stage is never swept clean.
Try! And Try! And Dry the cry!
The rooms are missing home, left home.

(cont'd)

XLII.

OLYMPUS ZWEI UND SIEBZIG (cont'd)

They're dead! They're gone!
The threshold feels their feet no more.
The games have ended! --- Torches pass!
But some receive it back
from having passed it on at birth.
They're dead! They're gone! The torch remains a sign:
A symbol frustrated and castrated, with only rime to cool
its burning pain.

XLIII.

PARADOX

I am not running away
but I must be traveling on.
And if I'm not moving ahead,
I must be running away.

I guess I'm mixed up
with different words for other thoughts;
but different thoughts are wrong
with other words.

How can I write more beautiful words
than the song that I hear?
How can I say more wonderful thoughts
than those that I feel in the music I see?

How can I touch more tenderly now
that you're mine and I hold you complete?
Well, maybe you know, more likely than I,
that we're closer than when we had wished to be one.

I guess I'm mixed up
with different words for other thoughts;
but different thoughts are wrong
with other words.

I am not moving ahead
so I must be running away;
but if I'm not running away,
I must be traveling on.

I love you still.

XLIV.

PARENT- CHILD / CHILD - PARENT

Please don't look at me and throw up both your hands
     and say you do not understand !
You make me feel you couldn't care to learn or help
     with what confuses me.

I need you, though I cannot ask --- You've got to know somehow.
You must help me scale the walls of emptiness.
     My goals have not begun to be, that worries me a lot.
I've got to get direction somewhere,
so I cling to friends and groups
going up or down and lost like me, or losing out.

You see, it doesn't matter to where I'm off.
You don't try much to be a friend. It frightens you I guess.
You offer rules and doubts of faith,
and all of those I break and burn and bury under fragile hopes,
while stuttering and shuddering in my tomb.

Didn't you grow up yet either? Maybe you would also like to play
my childlike games to learn what lies ahead,
or would you rather stay away?
It's hard to tell. I've known your life and cannot take what comes.
You peddle empty focus and you meddle in my dreams.

You make yourself out someone, yet you're lost and hopeless
just like me.
How can that be, when you're supposed to know it all?
I'm finding out you really don't. You're scared that I might know.
Don't worry though, just take it easy and you'll know
I love you even though you're weak.

Tell me that you're lost in knowing me.
We'll help each other in my need.
But don't give up – throw up your hands – How can I follow that?
It leads me nowhere, there I've been, and am until you lead.
Should I instead lead you to know and help me in my need?

(cont'd)

XLIV.

PARENT – CHILD / CHILD – PARENT   (cont'd)

Don't try to bridge a thing! There's distance! Leave it there.
It's good to know that you're beyond me. It's healthy if I learn
to stumble where you've been and as you did.
Don't be like me, for that's no path to follow.
I need your strength, but show me friendship, love,
and I'll love you, though I cannot say.
You'll just have to know, that's all.

My being good, or bad, or lost, is all the same to me.
You must be there to help me out.
Embrace me. Love me. Please. Please. Please.

PASSING FUTURES

What are you up to, Kay Louise?
You left us alone when you decided to leave.
We're depressed and thinking of you, Kay Louise.
Think of us too, but don't be sad because we're blue.

Where are you off to, Kay Louise?
You think you'll write when times are free?
We're doing a lot of living, thinking of you all the time.
Your supper prayers are silent, an empty table place in line.

> Did you have to go without me?
> Did you have to go alone?
> Did I let you down or lose you, Kay Louise?
> Are you coming soon, back home?

We've heard nothing from you, Kay Louise.
We've seen signs of passing futures,
but no signs of your warm smile and bubbly humor.
Earth and memories cause a fading light,
but still a candle glows dearest Kay.

> Did you have to go without me?
> Didn't I deserve a chance
> To say goodbye and wish you well?
> Did you have to go alone?
> Did I let you down or lose you, Kay Louise?
> Are you coming soon, back home?

We've heard nothing from you, Kay Louise.
We've seen signs of passing futures,
But no signs of your warm smile.
Earth and memories cause a fading light,
But still a candle glows for you.

> A toute a l'heure.

XLVI.

PEACE AT LAST

I found my lucky penny today.
I found my one-in-a-million with you.

I lost myself in the stars today.
I lost my love when it went to you.

Our hopes were dashed in our faces today.
The world-on-a-string tied itself in our knot.

Our time came along in a flash.
We fell in love forever today.

PLANNING DREAMS

A year, a day, a decade, a month ---
      What makes the difference?
Content or depressed --- It all stands on greed.

      His discipline, his organization,
            his guide for life,
      His faith in providence, his wish for order
            His need for nothing

His empty rules have let him fall.

      So he lays his plans for the future
            across an abyss of sagging tentacles.
      Reaching --- still grasping --- a bit beyond touching
            Groping --- still hoping --- for one to come true.

      Dreams he denies --- says they never existed.
            Just happen to be there if luck finds his plan.
      Though luck missed his calling,
            and dreaming, he did none.
      His plans don't come true.

He wants them --- He needs them --- His aging hands grieve
      for the looked-for, sought-after, what he still needs.
No end coming soon, with the mornings still clinging
      to afternoons, searching for orders to fill.

            Nothing really to hang on to,
            so go out and fall in love today.
            Believe. Please give and receive a
            someone falling in love with you.

XLVIII.

POINT OF NO RETURN

You're at the bottom of your rock
      and the rope you live on has come to an end.
Your life has been snagged and snarled
      in a maze of in's and out's, up's and down's, you're bound up.

So you tug and unravel.
      You think you've won battles;
But the war rages on in your heart,
      Never telling you --- Life's a dream!
Never knowing your pain's a scheme
      lost in the numbered grains of sand.
The umbrellas have closed --- you're on fire!

Your touch is lost. Your ship's a wreck.
You're sinking, but no one surrounds you.
The line you receive is a final relief.
You're out! Struck Away --- It's your day!

Now you're gone. Now you're done.
No one else comes along.
It's your want. It was always your way.
So you look at the end,
With a glance to the front,
Neither longer, nor shorter --- the way.

Now Get Up and Return. What's your problem? Go.

XLIX.

REFLECTION

It used to be today.
Now it's years ago.

It used to be I love you.
Now it's loved you so.

It used to be I'll see you soon;
But now it's time has flown.

It used to be remember me;
But now I've lost your name.

It used to be existence.
Now it's empty space.

    Who was I
    Now that you're gone?
    I can't remember me,
    Without you there to see.

    Reflection comes from others' eyes,
    acknowledgement within;
    but mortal men let loose the blame
    when lost and loose and tame.

L.

ROMAN PERMANENCE

Sunny blue Rome and the rain-swept

forever-form of the past, for the future

we stand in the gaze --- always still.

SATURDAY'S CURSE

Five weeks ago we parted.
                    I'll always hate Saturdays.
Your love has not returned.

Four weeks ago I wondered,
                    now what should I do today?
I'm desperate for someone to talk to,
                    but Saturday left me alone.

Three weeks ago I wrote you.
                    I asked what have you been doing.
I cried 'cause I'm lonely and need you.
                    Long Saturdays passing so slow.

Two weeks ago I waited.
                    I prayed you would call me or come.
You stayed away and I need you.
                    Then Sunday passed Saturday by.

One week ago I heard you.
                    You wrote me! There's fresh air again.
Then reading it told me you've settled
                    for Saturdays with no return.

Now, Saturday, you have returned.
                    I've passed you before; now I'll stay.
Your time has assured me; it never can cure me;
                    I'll not make it worse.

I'll pass over Saturday's curse.

LII.

SEASONS OF WARMTH

All that I say could be all that I write
                        to one of you.
All that I think could be all that I look
                        to one of you.
All that I do could be all that I am
                        to one of you.

    To one of you, I am alone.
    To one of you, I am in love.
    To one of you, I am the one
    Who'll stay beyond winter's cold sun.

What I don't say could be what I don't mean
                        to one of you.
How I don't act could be how I won't stay
                        to one of you.
When I don't come could be where I won't be
                        with one of you.
And why I don't cry could be I don't belong
                        to one of you.

Who I am not could be what's got to be
                        to one of you.
Who I become could be what I am now
                        to one of you.
Who you can love could be what I've become
                        to one of you.
And who you don't need could be how I might be
                        to one of you.

    To one of you, I am alone.
    To one of you, I am in love.
    To one of you, I am the one,
    You'll keep after summer's begun.

(cont'd)

LII.

SEASONS OF WARMTH   (cont'd)

All that you say could be all that I mean
                              to one of you.
All that you want could be what I've been like
                              to one of you.
All that you'll give could be what I've not done
                              for one of you.
And all that we want could be we don't belong
                              to one of you.

            To one of us, someone's alone.
            To two of us, someone's in love.
            To three of us, someone's the one
            I'll end up in springtime, undone.

LIII.

SELF DESTRUCT

Today, I've left two years behind.
Today, I've no more tears to find.
Now broken schemes and mended dreams
are floating closer to the ground.

The agony's somewhat subdued.
The pity for the self is through.
Now parting distance deems itself
a fine companion for the dance.

Tomorrow searches through the haze
of plans for pain, paid off in days
filled with the wished-for emptiness,
sought out to punish more --- not less.

SELFISH PITY

I cannot take the holidays.
I'd rather be alone.
The family ties of binding times
Reflect the warmth of what was home.

I cannot take the holidays.
I'd rather be alone.
The lonely hurt can do no harm.
The numbness fills the empty warm.

I cannot take the holidays.
I'd rather leave them far
away from thinking of what's passed,
together linking what's to last.

Holidays have changed meaning.
I cannot take the new.
The old fed out to be devoured
by differences, both false and true.

LV.

SERVE THE PUBLIC

Beware of the public whom you serve,

for they will kill you for your kindness.

SOUL GAME (1972)

Soul is the name of the game, my man.
Soul is the name of the game.
If you ain't got soul, you ain't got nothin'.
Soul is the name of the game.

You see, many folk claim they're got it, but they don't.
At least the ones who say they do --- definitely don't.
They're established and they couldn't
Don't really want to and they can't
Come out of their secure cocoon.
So they play at being soulful
Making claims of bridging the gap;
But if they did, they wouldn't need to
Talk about knowin where it's at.

What about the guy who hoots at hair
And laughs at clothes some people wear
Then tells his kids he understands
To come to him for a helping hand.

His attitude is degradation.
He's actually a vice.

Soul comes from the heart
Open, moving, sincere, and warm
Humorous at times, to laugh at change
Sad more often, seeing what remains.
Organization, law and order --- Yes !
Violence, hatred and death --- No !
Sure it's rough to go all out
But isn't that what it's all about?

Soul is the name of the game, my man.
Soul is the name of the game.
So give your soul and name the game.
Sign your name and play the game.

LVII.

STILL USED

People can easily agree or disagree

with what was said by the famous dead,

since the famous dead cannot threaten

or jeopardize such people's positions

or leadership grapplings and misstatements,

by repudiation.

LVIII.

TAKE CARE OF MY DAD

What is one man . . . but a guardian of my memory?

What is one man . . . I spend a thought within his light.

What is one place . . . except it empties now, another life.

What is one space . . . I look for no one to replace.

What is one man . . . His light goes on though dimmed by lack
of pulse.

What is one man . . . His careful friendship sealed an eternal
bond.

What is one face . . . grown blank by distance, time, and no
embrace.

What is one trace . . . We need not think his spirit's been erased.

He passed away . . . a friend of mine.

& a good guy with mom.

LIX.

THE AUDIENCE

The best people are in the audience.

I don't care if they love me or hate me.

They came to say hello and be a part and they're the best.

THE LOVE (An Ode to Wives)

I love to kiss my woman/
    Love to hold her, squeeze her, love her.
I love to taste her sweetness/
    Love to make her know I want her.
I love to see her eyes aglow
    With pride that she's enchanting.
I love to hear her speak my name
    And call me to be near her.

        Call me fickle, eager, proud and daring.
        Call me greedy, even though I'm sharing.
        Call me anything you think or care to . . .
        But you'll know that when you're finally through . . .

I love to dance, romance, and earn a chance/
    With her I need no second chance.
She's nice to touch, to smell her hair.
    I dig her being everywhere.
We drink and share the harvest wine.
    I want her just to say "You're Mine."
I watch her walk with head held high
    And I love to hold her thigh to thigh.

        Call me fickle, eager, proud and daring.
        Call me greedy, even though I'm sharing.
        Call me anything you think or care to . . .
        But you'll know that when you're finally through . . .

I love to kiss my wife/
    love to hold her, squeeze her, love her.
I love to taste her sweetness/
    Love to make her know I want her.
I love to see her eyes aglow
    With pride that she's enchanting.
I love to hear her speak my name
    And call me to be near her.

. . . .

THE HALLOWEEN MOON

The Halloween moon is a magic moon
and if it shines on you during Halloween night,
you will surely be strong, you will surely be bright.
For the spirits from heaven make your life bright.

The Halloween moon is a magic moon.
It's a magic light and if it shines on you during Halloween
night, your bowl will be full. Your feet will be light.
And your spirit will fly like a star on its flight.

The heavens above and the streets down below,
where no witches will get you,
they will run from the sight
of the Halloween moon and its magic light.

If you are lucky to sleep in the Halloween light
of the moon in your room, on your covers so tight,
let it warm you tonight. Let it ever be bright.
For the Halloween moon makes your future so bright.

LXII.

THE LECTURER

He talks so much that we don't have to think,

Other than to dream,

Other than to scheme,

Other than to doubt,

Other than to wonder why

we came at all

or paid the fee

when we can see

we don't agree

with what he says

or thinks of us.

His condescension labels us.

His patronizing stifles we

who eagerly seek truth.

We close the book.

The stigma lingers.

Oh, education come our way,

but lecturer, do not delay

our progress in the class of life.

Get off your past with us today.

Our futures will not wait !

LXIII.

THE LETTER FROM PAUL TO MY SON

It's time to believe in something
Take care of yourself
We have a son who has been born revived
You have a second life
Believe in something beyond your own selfishness
Don't waste it
It's a gift, this life, don't waste it
I was a party boy once. It's so easy. Don't throw it away
This second life of yours
I did.
He passed away his life but is still here.
Beyond himself, beyond all others, he needs to teach how to be here
to the listening, watching few.
Now it's your time.
Find out what to do now. You have eighty years.
Life is a 300 year lesson – But we only have 100 years to learn it.
So what are you going to do with it now? Don't waste it.
Overcome it with dignity
Persevere. Big challenge.
What do you want to do/be/contribute?
What do you want to teach your children?
&
That is what you must now teach yourself.
Persevere. Big challenge.
Wake up; otherwise, say shame on me and ask:
What do I do now?
Meditate. Medicate. Heal Yourself.
Use all forms East and West, but don't get hustled.
The Creator. HE. Gives us all this potential.
So, what are you going to do with it?
Overcome it
Big Challenge.
Now it's your time.
The world says that's great friend - But if
you don't do it - We don't care.
You have been granted a second life to absorb the first and learn
beyond your own selfishness.
Figure it out. Get Well.
Love

LXIV.

THEN I CAN SAY

If love is the comfort I feel when I hold you tight
If love is the warmth that I feel when you're in my sight
If love is the strength that I feel when you're in my arms
If love is the peace I receive from your natural charm,

    Then I can say that I'm really in love
    for I've said it before without feeling a thing
    and I'll never betray what "I Love You" means,
    with it comfort and strength, with its power and peace.

If love is using time to think of time still left to spend
If love is taking sides with no intending to offend
If love is smiling shyly thinking of you through the day
If love is feeling safe that we're not trapped, but want to stay,

    Then I can say that I'm really in love
    for I've said it before without feeling a thing
    and I'll never betray what "I love you" means,
    with its comfort and strength, with it power and peace.

If love is knowing someone doesn't mind your being wrong
If love is solving problems knowing someone's there and along
If love is gaining confidence by sensing someone's faith
If love is touching gently, with no fear that we might break,

    Then I can say that I'm really in love
    for I've said it before without feeling a thing
    and I'll never betray what "I love you" means
    with its comfort and strength, with its power and peace.

THE THEATRE
(An Ode to Lauren Bacall)

The theatre, the theatre, the theatre's my bag.
The theatre, the theatre, gives no one time to drag.

You don't stop while you wait.
You work and you work.
It doesn't owe you a break.
You work and you work.

The theatre, the theatre, love and hate, tears and joy
The theatre, the theatre, pride and pain, push and strain

The theatre, the theatre, talent cries, sadness looms.
The theatre, the theatre, strength remains, ends the glooms.

You don't give up. You don't say quit.
You work and you strive.
You're happy just being a part of it.
You work and you starve.

The theatre, the theatre, friends and faith, body and soul
The theatre, the theatre, laugh hello, never grow old.

LXVI.

THE USA --- A NEVER ENDING DISCOVERY

Shenango -- Durango
Going to the east through the middle from the west
Venango county line is mine
and Barkeyville is a Greentown twine,
but I can't rest now 'cause I'm in the wrong lane.

DuBois 16-66 --- Skeleton lying on the edge
as the pipelines bury themselves in the woods.
Tree houses watch us pass --- as Carole's mood changes.

Sideburns and Platinum are out for the holy ride
in the shiny red pick-up, they're close.
Exit 5, P A 38 --- Reflection calls out 41
and safe to leave at 35.

Big semi says they're the finest and they're edible.
Black crow picks the meat from the rib,
and the pure Allegheny currents by.

Fire tower number 2 calls a hundred dollar throwaway
a sin and a crime;
but people pay to pray here anyway.

Pines settle warmly round hilltop houses and valley-bottom
homes,
but the building farms and human forms
have abandoned the handiwork and the earthwork
and stolen it in an erosion flood to the city.
Now the blue creeks and the canoe brooks
wander and wonder through the crumble.
Especially now, the wolf's head need not stop short.

My overhead bridge guides emergency radar
and steps by the paths of express.
The calm isn't with me.
It's down there on 80 different rocks and puddles and half-paved
bike runs...,
and pine cones lie undisturbed by my eye-contact light.

(cont'd)

LXVI.

THE USA --- A NEVER ENDING DISCOVERY   (cont'd)

The shrubs reach out for me
and wave: Please Adore Me.
The Corsica story's brand new,
and deer step out bravely --- alive and abruptly,
they bump into our path
and the treasure's a pool on a concrete lake

The men of the earth bring a cool basic need to the East.
They push it and pull it, and sunny-blue move it.
They're the best and they know it,
and don't hog to show it.

Food - Lodging - and Gas
with a phone to call home --- I don't need
with a clear field to steeples
above the dead trees.
Yes, those toothpick soldiers peer down from their tops,
while their silhouettes command our gazing at them in awe,
as though they stand poised on the verge of attack;
and we, in helpless fear,
though less afraid of death than life,
we melt within their shadow.

Then Shenandoah spots a ring of buildings around a fire,
and homeward, Buckhorn exits with a tease, a hint, a heart
of warmth, to show the way.

Old October Mountain scales the Hickory Run
And fades out with the sun. Be at peace.

LXVII.

THIS I LIKE
(Are you kidding me?)

This I like --- just to be quiet
No pressures and no place to go
No one pressing for what I think
Or where I want to go.

Yes, the door goes shut.
Nobody's left behind.

Oh, this I like --- I call on you
It's quiet talk, a warm and gentle touch.
We don't demand.
We know we've got so much.

No slow routines
No habits stuck in grooves.

Yes, this I like --- no boring days
With doubts: What did I do? What?

I'm fast asleep
No one to kiss goodnight

Should I get up?
When will my life be right?

Think about it.
What did you do? Are you kidding me?

Too late Mister.
You lose.

LXVIII.

TIME LAPSE

It's three-thirty
and I'm wondering
if I'll be alive at forty-five
or somewhere lost beyond the sea.

It's four, I've left,
no more to think
or doubt when I'm fifteen.
And when I'm back to thirty,
will I know where I have been?

A quarter passed,
one-half a distance
yet to be fulfilled;
but when the hour strikes its chime,
will I be there on time?

On-time's frustrated now and then,
or when it used to be,
for then it's over,
nothing lost,
or gained, but what I see.

The time is gone;
It's coming gone,
Or lost and gone forever.

LXIX.

TOO SOON

She loves me now.
What more can I ask.
I want her now.
We need it to last.

If I can't hold your attention,
then I don't dare try to hold your life.
If you can't hold your deflection
then you can't say you see only me.

If we fall down in our love for sharing,
and we look for another spark,
then we won't make it in our caring
as we did when we made our start.

    Take a look
    Make the switch
    Take a jump
    Break the stitch

If we have to take that look
just for interest, curious, see,
then we'll possibly have to admit
time still owes us out being free.

If we're bound to stop our head,
holding tight by the other's dread,
then our natural trust and faith
is a fraud and a bawd and a waste.

If doubt creeps around for a look,
then we must recognize what it takes.
If doubt steals away with some time,
the touch doesn't mean it will break.

She loves me now
What more can I ask
I want her forever
We need it to last.

(cont'd)

LXIX.

TOO SOON (cont'd)

It's not necessarily trust at stake
It's not necessarily youth
It's not necessarily age at length
It's faith, understanding and us.

If love ebbs and flows away,
it will tell us in less than a day.
Without taking sides, it has never been blunt.
It has warned us and shown us before.

Rooting and spreading so high,
the waves of our love spread the growth.
It's never too soon to commit to our love.
We want more and see more. Let's go !

LXX.

TORONTO TIMETABLE

Oh, I'm up here making my fame and fortune.
That's what It's all about.
My family's O'K and I just couldn't stay.
I had to make it, you know, my way.

> Isn't it a pity to see a lost dog,
> all skinny and dirty?
> But what about a kid?

Oh, I'm up here flying in clouds and formations.
Well, that's where it's supposed to be.
My friends are all great and I just want to make
them know I'm not late, that's all.

> Isn't it too bad about war everywhere someone
> dares to be different?
> Watch your friends when their green is your grass.

Oh, I'm up here on my own, not remembering home
and that's how far I've gathered time.
I'm learning my turn is not measured by lines,
and the distance no measure of mine.

> It's a shame he's a drunk on the stoop of despair
> near the trap door to food and decay.
> What about freedom anyway?

Oh, I'm up here looking back, from the outside, looking in.
That's the time I use to cover space.
The revelation's clear to me.
It's time for "now or never". It's time to set a pace.

> It's disgraceful he's off in his own little world /
> Made an outcast by society.
> Is there any room for me?

LXXI.

TREASURE HUNT

Spring doesn't last all year.
Love isn't fresh for a lifetime.
Go to sleep now and don't think about it.

With her ear near my ear, she can hear that I love her.
With her breast on my chest, she can count on my life.
And my lips read the tips of her fingers to tell me
She's touching my thoughts without speaking a line.

    Sleep doesn't end the strength.
    Dark isn't blinding the warmth.
    Go to love now and don't talk about it.

With her eyes, no goodbyes, she can welcome --- I love her.
With her love and my need, she can take all my heart.
And we're growing and coming together, together,
Fresh, strong and forever / no slept over thoughts.

    Seasons bring fresh new strength.
    Love goes beyond new and shiny.
    Go to time now and don't wait for signals.

With her backing to be, throughout time, destiny
With her children of beauty, a proud line of love
And they're loving her, loving me, growing in family
Caring and offering eternity.

    Prizes don't bring fame and fortune.
    Memories don't sidestep the pain.
    Go together now and don't limit yourselves.

TRY IT ONCE AGAIN

When a woman cries for me,
I feel it and I love her so;
but when I have to cry for her,
it hurts so much I cannot look.

When a woman gives me love
I want to take it close and spend it all;
but when I want to give her love,
I burden her with taking me.

    I don't know what I'm saying
    or what I mean to make so clear.
    I thought I did, but don't believe I do.
    I'll try it once again.

When a woman tells me she is mine,
I want to tell her don't, it shouldn't be;
but when I shy away from yes,
she gives me all and takes me too.

When a woman talks of years from now,
I picture pleasant memories still ahead;
but when I think of what she'll get
I beg her stop, but stay for now.

    I don't know what I'm saying
    or what I mean to make so clear.
    I thought I did, but don't believe I do.
    I'll try it once again.

When a woman gives her life and love,
her years and self, and eyes of time,
my thoughts become a sense of growth,
contesting what I'm worth.

(cont'd)

LXXII.

TRY IT ONCE AGAIN (cont'd)

When a woman makes me feel as though
an anger's swelling in my blood,
I recognize a full emotion
trapped in search of losing her.

    I don't know what I'm saying,
    or why I must be clear.
    I thought I did, but don't believe I do.
    I'll try one final time.

When a woman says she loves me
and I crumble under peaceful eyes,
I know she owes me nothing,
but I'll pay her full before I die.

    Yes. Nice. Always Choose Love.

LXXIII.

UNEMPLOYMENT

Mail in your application.
They'll see what they can do.
They'll buy your heart and sell your soul.
There's nothing you can do.

Mail in your application.
Don't bother with a call.
They'll tell you there's no work today.
You'll have to wait, that's all.
      Well, I've waited and I'm tired.
      I've waited and I'm through.
      I'm good for work; I'll choose my own,
      Hard tellin' what I'll do.
"We'll call you when we need you.
We'll call you when there's room."
There's room to wait out on the street,
With hunger, gloom and doom.

"We've got your application.
We've got your number too."
You've got my name; I've got my time.
A number, waiting in some line !
      Well, I've waited and I'm tired.
      I've waited and I'm through.
      I'm good for work; I'll choose my own.
      Hard tellin' what I'll do.
"We've read your application.
We've noticed you've trained well.
We're looking now. We're doing our best;
But you'll have to take a test."

"The test will be one month from now.
There'll also be a fee.
We'll take your cash and hope you pass,
Or a longer wait it'll be."

      Well I've waited and I'm tired !
      I've waited and I'm through.
      I'm good for work ! I'll choose my own !
      Watch Out ! I'm warning you !

LXXIV.

VANITY

If I make a statement and you hear me, what I've said,
    what care I if it's written down / for isn't communication
    first between two / and carried to three and four and
    so on, by repetition and addition, until everyone
    knows --- who cares?

If I smolder and smoke, and maybe burst into flame, what
    care I if you warm yourself in my heat / for doesn't light
    travel faster then warmth / and you'll see what I say / and
    then warm yourself / and from your own light, warm others?

Why should I have thoughts of being handsome in your eyes /
    for that's your worry and not mine.
And what care I of vain attempts at self beautification / my
    body is not ruled by you, but me.
And too, if you're repulsed by my appearance, that is not
    my doing either, now is it / for you have set up your own
    repulsive attitude toward me, which makes you repulsive.
So, break your habit, or be broken / for I will not disappear
    and I don't plan on making any changes soon.

        The entrance to the future is the death
            of my past, though I've
            used it and couldn't hold it,
            I still look forward to my age
            when I can become young again
            and shed the lies of moving
            ahead, and finally tell the truth.

        Don't we all?

LXXV.

WELCOME TO NEW YORK CITY

They come like the snow

and then melt with the blows

they receive

from the heat of the push.

Don't miss the view of the city

as you go over the bridge.

You Are Always Welcome in NYC !

LXXVI.

WE MUST

We must keep caring
We must keep sharing . . . .

We must keep knowing
We must keep showing . . . .

We must keep praying
We must keep saying . . . .

We must keep thinking
We must keep linking . . . .

We must keep sighing
We must keep trying . . . .

We must keep using
We must keep choosing . . . .

We must keep blending
Never ending . . . . love.

LXXVII.

WHAT ARE THEY DOING

(The Child Asks Mommy/Daddy)

What are they doing?

      They're watching the ocean.

What is it doing?

      Oh, it's coming in and going out.

Does it bring anything with it?

      No.

Does it take anything out with it?

      No.

Do they think it is going to?

      Well, sometimes they do.

Is that why they're waiting?

      No, they just come out here to relax and think.

Think about what?

      Oh, I don't know --- about what they're doing I guess.

What are they doing?

      . . . .

LXXVIII.

WITHIN WITHOUT

Shoot me down
Warm me up
I'm lying here in space.
Gently cutting through the haze,
I'm feeling much farther away.

Sensation's gone. It's tougher now.
Receiving pain and fright
I've caught a glimpse of nowhere.
I've been here once before.

I can't get out. It's choking me.
The rings are colored and sharp.
They're a twisting, cutting, engulfing mist.
I've lost my sight and touch.

I'm upside down, I'm inside out.
I've turned within without.
Please capture me. I'm lost again,
A missing space, misplaced.

Please find me in and outside too.
Please find me round the space.
Please know that I am in your circle
Knowing we are there by Grace.

YOU SHOULD FALL IN LOVE FOREVER
AT LEAST ONCE
EVERYDAY
1

She walks by, so beautifully shy
And she hears me carefully sigh.
I long for her, not knowing why,
Though I hope she's thinking I'll try
To be hers, to be hers 'til I die
And we're quietly not telling lies.

She is still. She is shy.
She is standing close by.

Then I walk to meet her and smile to greet her
And warmly look in her eyes.
She turns away bashfully, looking back carefully,
Knowing it may be a lie;
But she sees no dangerous eye
And she smiles and answers my sigh.

She is still. She is shy.
She is waiting close by.

So we walk so casually
Talk so easily
Not knowing time's going by.

She's alone for the evening.
I'm free for a lifetime.
I want her. There's no use to lie.

She is still. She is shy.
First she smiles. Then she sighs.

She is still. She is shy.
Now we laugh --- and we'll try.

She is still. I am shy.
We cannot say goodbye.

LXXX.

YOU SHOULD FALL IN LOVE FOREVER
AT LEAST ONCE
EVERYDAY
2

Sweet Melinda, I cannot forget
the way you touched my hand while you changed my life.

And Melinda, how you waited on my wishes
with your "What'll it be here?" just like coffee or tea.

Oh Melinda, I would joy to see
your sparkling hair flow freely,
and flower over bosoms so soft;
and tenderly I'd read your eyes
and meet them with my lips.

And Melinda, though apart we'd stay,
our closeness would stay on,
reviving still unheard of thoughts
and memories to come.

My Melinda, you are seen but once,
and once met face to face.
you cannot say you love me,
and I cannot know you're mine;
but when we meet in truer light,
we'll not hide life within.

For Melinda, know me when I come.
We will pray on our love to be true;
and knowing me, you'll keep me near
and we'll love, my Melinda, you.

LXXXI.

YOU SHOULD FALL IN LOVE FOREVER
AT LEAST ONCE
EVERYDAY
3

And as we say in so many ways
you should see love, find love, meet love
in every way and form it shows itself,
for it will surely be everywhere, everyday.

You must notice it and embrace it and give it away.
It's there for you and it's in you to have for others.
It's the strength of you to give to others.
It's the strength in you to notice love in others, Everyday.

Someone is always giving and needing love.
Someone is always hearing and speaking compassion.
Someone is always knowing and speaking tenderness.
And you are the one who knows yours best.

Do it and you will see. Do it and you well know
that you can love this one and that,
as well as be loved by that one and this.
Who knows but that he and she will fall in love forever
everyday too, thanks to you.

LXXXII.

YEAR OF "SWEET SIXTEEN" + 1000

2016 To 3016

Be in love with the future.

Be in love with what you leave behind.

Plan everyday for what you drop in your path.

Sow some love sincerely Everyday.

Plant it. Grow it. Fertilize it. Nourish it. Harvest it. Enjoy.

Love is yours for Giving and Accepting Everyday.

Leave/Give at least Ten percent For/To others

As a Blessing / For a Blessing

8/20/2016 & 4/12/2014
+1000

Forever and Beyond

LXXXIII.

A WORTHY PERSON

You will surely meet a very valuable, lovable

and worthy person in your life Everyday.

And: You will become a very valuable, lovable and

Worthy person in somebody's life Everyday.

Stay Tuned & Pay Attention! ☺

Love ya,

Bruce

LXXXIV.

POSTSCRIPT: IT ALL COMES FULL CIRCLE (1972-2016)

Do you think that people are trying to put away their hate and lying?
    To put and end to all of this dying,
    do you think that people are trying?
    You gotta make them wanna start tryin.

You ask me what-in-the-world can I do. I'm only one, so what can I do?
    Well you're forgettin me and that makes two.
    Look around and you'll see quite a few.
    We're together.
    Let's see what we can do.

Do you think that people really wanna try to understand and love you?
    Think they really care to wanna help themselves begin to try to?
    You gotta help them begin to try to.
    You gotta help them begin to try to.

        Show them love is not a thing for buyin.
        Well that's just another way of lyin.
        We gotta put an end to this hate and dyin.
        It's been so long since I've seen smilin.

Do you think we'll ever have everyone respectin love and lovin anyone,
    no matter what s/he is or who s/he is or what s/he has done?
    You know there's lots of good in everyone.
    You gotta find that good in everyone.

Do you think that people are tryin to put away their hate and lyin?
    To put an end to all of this dyin,
    Do ya think that people are tryin?

You gotta make them wanna start tryin!
    You gotta make them wanna start tryin!
        You gotta make them wanna start tryin . . . .

        Show them love is not a thing for buyin.
        Well that's just another way of lyin.
        We gotta put an end to this hate and dyin.
        It's been so long since I've seen smiling.

Bruce Sanford grew up in the farmlands of Greentown and North Canton, Ohio. He was the little brother among five sons and daughters of Karl and Ruth Sanford. Bruce is currently a full-time faculty member of the City University of New York, teaching entry-level mathematics on the Tribeca campus of the Borough of Manhattan Community College.

A graduate of Ashland University in Ohio and also of Hofstra University in Hempstead, Long Island, New York, Bruce has traveled through theater, music, writing, and teaching to bring you this Book of Poetry & Lyrics, in addition to his already published children's songs book of music and lyrics in 2015 and also his already published Universal Children's Prayers book in 2013.

Bruce has also produced and published his Remembering poster tribute to our USA veterans, victims, servers and sufferers, reflecting our wars, conflicts, 9/11, Boston, Fort Hood, Benghazi, Beirut, Orlando, etc., available on his website—SanfordPublishing.com as well as his large Sanford Circles® Of Numbers poster. Stay tuned for his math book and video teaching of six years of continuity content from Times Tables Into Algebra, a math board game (MultipleChoices®), drama and music productions/publications, along with an audio book and CD production of the children's songs, produced and performed by himself and his daughter, Rebecca Ruth Sweeney.

Jeanny Humphrey is a native New Jerseyan from Hamilton, trained in professional graphic design and printing with substantial years of studio, photo lab, and counter experience with Photo Haven in Lawrenceville. She is now working as a full-time graphic artist and printer with Future Signs & Creations Inc. of Trenton. Having been an integral part of the Sanford Children's Prayers Book of 2013, and also, being the graphic design and formatting artist of his 2012 Remembering poster tribute to our USA veterans, victims, servers, and sufferers, available on SanfordPublishing.com, Jeanny continued providing her valuable expertise in Sanford's 2015 book of children's songs and has once again been integral with the graphic formatting and enhancement artistry of the cover photos for this poetry and lyrics book.

About the Book

This book of poetry and lyrics is an ongoing set of love and
information statements and letters to all people
regarding the thoughts and feelings relating to Bruce Sanford's
experiences, the effects of world events, and references
throughout nearly six decades of his evolving life and living,
with still much more to come.

From his Greentown childhood in rural farmland near Canton, Ohio
to the honor of being enchanted by all five boroughs
of neighborhoods and people throughout New York City, and across
Liberty Harbor and out into the fields and farms and
along the shores of central New Jersey,
opinions, suggestions, information, and even some twists and turns
and pivots throughout this book.

From world and country and personal history, Bruce has steadfastly and
resolutely lived and portrayed the belief that there is always and
forever an impromptu and spontaneous love, in the moment, to or
from at least one person, and even more than one person, Everyday.
There are so many nice and special people on encounters
every single day. We should each watch and notice. We should absorb
and acknowledge that flicker of love and warmth,
that fleeting moment of knowing it just happened again, and again
and again, and even again but At Least Once, EVERYDAY !

"Simply Watch For IT and Notice and Please Enjoy and Pass It On ! ☺"

Printed in the United States
By Bookmasters